D1275181

ENERGY

ENERGY

A REFERENCE
FIRST BOOK

BY MELVIN BERGER
DRAWINGS BY
ANNE CANEVARI GREEN

A GROLIER COMPANY

FRANKLIN WATTS
NEW YORK | LONDON | TORONTO
SYDNEY | 1983

Photographs courtesy of:
Los Alamos Photo Laboratory: p. 9;
Department of Energy: pp. 13, 21, 45, 59, 61, 67, 80, 82, 83;
Argonne National Laboratory: pp. 15, 32, 58;
National Archives: p. 19; Tennessee Valley Authority: pp. 23, 46;
The New York Public Library Picture Collection:
pp. 24, 27, 28, 32, 33, 36, 37, 78, 90;
U.S. Army Corps of Engineers: p. 25; Green Bay Packers: p. 30;
NASA: pp. 31, 55; U.S. Air Force: p. 47;
University of California Lawrence Livermore Laboratory: pp. 49, 54;
Princeton University: p. 53; n.c.: p. 62;
Sinclair Oil Corp.: pp. 68, 77;
Mobil Photo Library: p. 72;
The Aluminum Association: p. 76;
USAEC Grand Junction Office: p. 89.

Library of Congress Cataloging in Publication Data

Berger, Melvin.
Energy.

(A Reference first book)
Summary: A lexicon of terms relating to energy, from
active solar energy system, air conditioning, and
Alaskan pipeline, to wind turbine, windmill, and work.
1. Power resources—Dictionaries, Juvenile.
2. Power (Mechanics)—Dictionaries, Juvenile.
[1. Power resources—Dictionaries.
2. Power (Mechanics)—Dictionaries]
I. Green, Anne Canevari, ill. II. Title. III. Series.
TJ163.23.B47   1983   621.042′0321   82-16083
ISBN 0-531-04536-6

Copyright © 1983 by Melvin Berger
All rights reserved
Printed in the United States of America
5   4   3   2   1

ENERGY

A

ACTIVE SOLAR ENERGY SYSTEM. A system for collecting, storing, and using solar energy for space heating, water heating, or cooling. Pumps, fans, or other mechanical devices are used to distribute the solar heat. In such a system a source of energy in addition to the sun, such as electricity, is needed to operate the fans and pumps. In contrast, a passive solar energy system requires no additional energy source; the natural or structural parts of the building passively store and distribute the solar heat. *See also* PASSIVE SOLAR ENERGY SYSTEM; SOLAR COLLECTOR; SOLAR ENERGY; and SOLAR ENERGY SYSTEM.

AIR CONDITIONING. A system for controlling the temperature, humidity (moisture), and quality of air in a room or building. To cool the air of a room during hot weather, the compressor in the air conditioner condenses a gas and changes it into a liquid state. This releases heat into the outside air. The liquid is then expanded, or evaporated, which turns it into a gas again. This gas absorbs heat from the air in the room and produces a cooling effect. Fans blow the cool air around the room. Moisture in the air condenses on the coils of the air conditioner and drips into a pan. Filters in the air conditioner clean the air. Energy is needed to operate the compressor and fans. *See also* COMPRESSOR; CONDENSATION; and EVAPORATION.

ALASKAN PIPELINE. An 800-mile-long (1,300-km) pipeline that carries oil from the oilfields around Prudhoe Bay on the Arctic Ocean in northern Alaska to the port of Valdez on its southern coast. Completed in 1977, the Alaskan Pipeline was very difficult to build. It is aboveground for about 400 miles (640 km) and crosses twenty large rivers, three hundred streams, and three mountain ranges. It is also called the Trans-Alaska Pipeline. *See also* PIPELINE.

ALPHA PARTICLES. Particles emitted by certain radioactive substances; also, the nucleus of the helium atom, which is made up of two protons and two neutrons bound together. An alpha particle is not a very penetrating form of radiation and can be stopped by a sheet of paper. *See also* RADIOACTIVITY.

ALTERNATE ENERGY SOURCES. Energy sources other than those most commonly used—petroleum, or oil, and natural gas. The alternate sources include nuclear, coal, and renewable sources, such as sun, wind, water, plants, and other biomass. Sometimes the term "alternate sources" is used to mean only the renewable sources. *See also* BIOMASS; ENERGY CONSERVATION; GEOTHERMAL ENERGY; HYDROELECTRIC ENERGY; RENEWABLE ENERGY SOURCES; SOLAR ENERGY; TIDAL ENERGY; WAVE ENERGY; and WIND ENERGY.

ANNUAL CYCLE ENERGY SYSTEM. An experimental year-round method of heating and cooling houses. The house is warmed in the winter by use of a heat pump to remove the heat from a large, insulated underground tank of water. This turns the water into ice. The ice is then stored to cool the house during the summer. The system saves at least 50 percent of the usual energy costs. *See also* HEAT PUMP.

ANODE. An electrode, or terminal, in certain electrical devices, such as batteries or cells. In a battery the positive terminal is called the anode. *See also* BATTERY and ELECTRODE.

ANTHRACITE. A hard, black coal. Anthracite usually produces about 25 million Btus per ton. *See also* BTU and COAL.

ATOM. The smallest unit of a chemical element. An atom cannot be broken apart by chemical means. Each atom has a central core, called the nucleus.

Inside the nucleus are two types of particles, protons and neutrons. Both have approximately the same mass. But protons have a positive electrical charge, while neutrons are electrically neutral.

Electrons are in orbit around the nucleus of the atom. They have less mass than either protons or neutrons and a negative electrical charge. The number of protons and electrons in an atom are usually the same. If they are not equal, the atom has either a positive or negative charge. Such an atom is called an ion. *See also* ELECTRON; ION; MOLECULE; NEUTRON; NUCLEAR FISSION; NUCLEAR FUSION; and PROTON.

ATOMIC BOMB. An explosive device, first tested in 1945, that is a powerful weapon of warfare. The atomic bomb, or A-bomb, as it is also known, is based on uncontrolled nuclear fission brought about by a chain reaction. Slower, controlled fission is now the main source of nuclear energy for peaceful purposes. *See also* CHAIN REACTION and NUCLEAR FISSION.

The world's first nuclear explosion, shown here, took place on a testing range in New Mexico in 1945.

ATOMIC ENERGY. Term once used to refer to the energy released by a nuclear reaction. The more current term is *nuclear energy*. *See also* NUCLEAR ENERGY.

ATOMIC ENERGY COMMISSION. The U.S. government agency formed to supervise and control the peaceful use of nuclear energy in the United States. In 1974 the Atomic Energy Commission was replaced by the Energy Research and Development Administration (ERDA) and the Nuclear Regulatory Commission (NRC). ERDA was replaced by the Department of Energy in 1977.

ATOMIC REACTOR. *See* NUCLEAR REACTOR.

B

BATTERY. A device that changes chemical energy into electrical energy.

A battery consists of one or more units, called cells. In each cell there is a positive and negative electrode, known respectively as the anode and cathode. These electrodes are separated by an electrolyte—a chemical com-

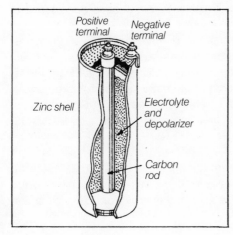

A battery

pound that conducts electricity. If a conductor or external circuit is connected to the electrodes, electrons will flow from the negative electrode (the cathode) through the electrolyte to the positive electrode (the anode).

The type of battery used in flashlights and portable radios is a dry cell. A dry cell produces electricity until all the chemical energy has been changed into electrical energy. The type of battery used in automobiles is called a storage battery. Storage batteries must first be charged by electricity. The battery stores this charge, then discharges it as needed. When a storage battery is being charged, the flow of electrons is reversed. The positive terminal is then the cathode, and the negative terminal is the anode.

BECQUEREL, ANTOINE HENRI (1852–1908). French scientist. Bequerel was the first to detect natural radioactivity. He announced his discovery in 1896, after noting that uranium was able to expose photographic film that was shielded from the light. Becquerel shared the 1903 Nobel prize in physics with Marie and Pierre Curie.

BETA PARTICLES. Particles emitted by certain radioactive materials. A beta particle with a negative charge is an electron; with a positive charge it is a positron. Beta particles can be stopped by a thin sheet of metal. *See also* RADIOACTIVITY.

BIOMASS. Material derived from living organisms, including ordinary plant matter, agricultural products, trees, seaweed, and animal manure. Because it uses sunlight, or solar energy, to grow the plants, biomass is considered a form of solar energy.

By means of special processes, biomass can be changed into various types of fuel. Biomass used for energy production has several benefits, such as aiding in waste disposal and cutting down on air pollution. A disadvantage is that it is costly to collect the huge amounts of biomass needed for large-scale energy production. One important goal of energy research is to grow plants that will be especially good sources of fuel and energy. *See also* BIOMASS CONVERSION and PHOTOSYNTHESIS.

BIOMASS CONVERSION. The process of changing biomass into a source of energy. The oldest and most obvious way is to burn substances such as wood. But now scientists are finding other ways to obtain energy from different types of biomass.

This plant burns garbage to produce steam for energy.

Biomass conversion can take place in several ways. The biomass can be placed in a sealed tank and heated to 662°F (350°C) while hydrogen gas is introduced. The hydrogen combines with carbon from the biomass and produces oil. Another approach is to shred and dry the biomass, then heat it to 932°F (500°C) in the absence of oxygen. The gases that are produced are condensed, and both oil and fuel gas are obtained.

Still another method, called anaerobic digestion, uses bacteria to decompose the biomass in the absence of air. Anaerobic digestion produces a gas containing about 65 percent methane, the main part of natural gas.

In the fermentation process certain kinds of biomass, such as grains or sugarcane, are allowed to ferment. This produces alcohol, which can be burned as a fuel or added to gasoline to make gasohol.

In some biomass conversion processes garbage is used to produce energy. Typically, garbage contains plant and animal matter along with inorganic wastes, such as metal, paper, plastic, and glass. Some of this waste can be burned as a fuel to produce energy. The rest can be removed and recycled. *See also* GASOHOL and RECYCLING.

BITUMINOUS. A soft coal that is either dark brown or black in color. Bituminous coal produces about 25 million Btus per ton. *See also* BTU and COAL.

BLACK LUNG DISEASE. A disabling respiratory illness that mostly strikes coal miners because of all the coal dust they breathe in as they work. The medical name is *anthracosis*.

BLACKOUT. A failure of either the generation or transmission of electrical power so that no electricity is available in a particular area for a while.

BOHR, NIELS (1885–1962). Danish physicist who devised the modern theory of the atom. Bohr was educated in Denmark and in England and worked in the United States during part of World War II. It was Bohr's contributions to an understanding of the nature of nuclear fission that made commercial nuclear fission—and the atomic bomb—possible. In 1922, Bohr received the Nobel prize in physics for his pioneering work in atomic physics.

BOILER. A container or vessel in which water is heated and changed to steam.

BOILING WATER REACTOR. A type of nuclear reactor. Water is used to cool the reactor. The heat from the reactor causes the water to boil. The steam goes directly to drive a turbine, is then converted back to water by cooling, and the water is pumped back to cool the reactor again. *See also* NUCLEAR REACTOR.

BREEDER REACTOR. A type of nuclear reactor that produces more nuclear fuel than it uses.

The breeder reactor uses plutonium and uranium 238 as its fuel. It does not have a moderator to slow the reactions down, as ordinary nuclear reactors do.

The result of this is that while the reactor is producing power by fissioning the plutonium, extra neutrons are also striking the uranium and coverting it to plutonium. The plutonium can later be "reprocessed," or used again, as fuel for nuclear reactions. Thus, in time, a breeder reactor can actually "breed" more fuel than it started out with.

This does not mean, however, that the breeder reactor is actually creating fuel. It is really just using and reusing the same fuel, each time extracting a little more of the fuel's energy potential.

In spite of their obvious advantages, breeder reactors have not been developed for use in the United States. The plutonium ''bred'' is enriched enough to be used for the making of bombs, and the government to this point has hoped to limit the spread of nuclear weapons by not making the fuel for them quite so available. There are breeder reactors in operation in Europe, however, especially in West Germany and France, and in Japan. *See also* NUCLEAR REACTOR.

The Argonne National Laboratory's Experimental Breeder Reactor II, near Idaho Falls, Idaho.

BRITISH THERMAL UNIT. *See* BTU.

BROWNOUT. A partial failure of either the generation or transmission of electrical power so that less electricity than normal is available in a particular area for a while.

BTU. Abbreviation for *British thermal unit.* It is the amount of heat needed to raise the temperature of 1 pound (0.45 kg) of water 1 degree Fahrenheit (0.6 degrees Celsius). One Btu is equal to 252 calories. The Btu is the standard unit of heat energy. *See also* CALORIE.

CALORIE. A standard measure of heat. It is the amount of heat needed to raise one gram of water one degree Celsius. One calorie is equal to approximately 1/250 Btu. *See also* BTU.

CALVIN, MELVIN (b. 1911). U.S. scientist. Calvin won the Nobel prize in chemistry in 1961 for discovering all of the separate reactions that occur during photosynthesis. In recent years he has been doing research on growing plants as sources of energy. *See also* BIOMASS CONVERSION and PHOTOSYNTHESIS.

CARBONIFEROUS PERIOD. The period of earth's history from approximately 400 to 300 million years ago. During this time large amounts of coal, as well as oil and natural gas, were formed in the earth. Also called the Coal Age. *See also* COAL.

CATHODE. An electrode, or the negative terminal, in certain electrical devices. In a battery, the negative terminal is called a cathode. *See also* BATTERY and ELECTRODE.

CHAIN REACTION. A reaction that keeps on going once it is started. The fission reaction in a nuclear reactor is an example of a chain reaction. As each atom is split, it releases neutrons, which split other atoms. This releases more neutrons that split more atoms, and so on.

CHEMICAL ENERGY. The energy stored in molecules, which are chains of atoms. When molecules are split apart, or when atoms combine to form molecules, energy may be released. During burning, the molecules of a piece of wood, for example, join with oxygen from the air. The result is combustion, with the release of heat and light energy.

COAL. A soft rock derived from plant matter that is a very important source of energy. Black or brown in color, it contains a large amount of the chemical element carbon. Coal is found buried in the earth. It looks smooth and polished. A close examination, though, may show remains, or fossils, of plants. The remains show that coal is a fossil fuel. It was formed from plants that grew on earth hundreds of millions of years ago. Many of the plants were huge and lived in thick forests and swamps. When these giant plants died, they fell into the swamps and formed a thick mass of decaying vegetable matter. The material, which was formed underwater where there was little oxygen, is called peat. Peat is the first step in the formation of coal.

Hundreds of millions of years passed. Layers of dirt and sand blew over the peat. New plants began growing on top. In some places the peat was completely covered with water. The heat and pressure gradually changed the peat into coal. Scientists estimate that it took about 6 feet (1.8 m) of dead plants plus millions of years to form a 1-foot (0.3-m) layer of coal.

There are two main types of coal. Hard coal is called anthracite. Soft coal is called bituminous.

Anthracite contains less burnable matter than bituminous because it was formed under greater pressure. It burns with almost no smoke. Most of America's anthracite coal is found deep under the earth's surface in eastern Pennsylvania.

Bituminous is the most plentiful and important coal for energy production. It is found in many areas of the United States. The largest beds, though, are located just west of the Appalachian Mountains, in a region that stretches from Ohio to Alabama.

Coal that is near the surface is usually removed by strip mining. Giant earth-moving equipment strips away the earth and rock covering the coal seam.

Explosives break up the coal. Power shovels then load it into huge trucks to be hauled away.

Coal that is far beneath the surface is removed by underground, or deep, mining. A hole is dug down to the coal seam. The miners use drilling and cutting machines to break the coal up. The coal is then loaded into cars and hauled up to the surface by elevator.

More than half of the electrical power in the United States is produced by burning coal as fuel. The heat from the burning coal is used to change water into steam. The steam turns turbines that then turn generators to create the electricity. An ounce (28 g) of coal can produce as much electricity as 100 tons of water falling 1 foot (0.3 m). Electricity-generating plants use over 260 million tons of bituminous coal every year.

In this World War I surface coal-mining operation, coal is being stripped away from a coal seam by a mechanical shovel and dumped into railroad cars for transportation to a power plant.

An estimated 3 trillion tons of coal lie under U.S. land. At present consumption rates, the supply could last us for nearly five thousand years. But not all of this coal can be dug up. And some types of coal produce unacceptable amounts of air pollution. The usable coal is believed to total about 300 billion tons. This is about a three-hundred-year supply at the present rate of use. Coal makes up 90 percent of our nation's reserves of fossil fuels. Natural gas makes up 4 percent and oil 3 percent.

The quality of a fuel depends on how much heat comes from burning a fixed quantity of it. For example, coal from the Western strip mines is cheap and plentiful. But it only produces three-quarters as much heat as coal from the Eastern deep mines.

The amount of the element sulfur in the coal is another important factor. If the sulfur content is high, burning the coal produces a great deal of air pollution. Certain laws forbid the burning of high-sulfur coal unless the smoke is cleaned before it is released into the air. *See also* SCRUBBER.

COAL GASIFICATION. The production from coal of a gas that can be burned as fuel. In the nineteenth and early twentieth centuries, almost all fuel gases—water gas, producer gas, and coal gas, for example—were made from coal. However, as natural gas, which is cheaper and hotter-burning, became available, the use of fuel gases diminished greatly. Then, in the 1970s, as supplies of oil became unreliable and prices soared, and natural gas supplies seemed to be dwindling, the interest in gases made from coal increased again.

The simplest and cheapest coal gasification method is the Lurgi process. The coal is broken down, or crushed, into tiny pieces. Hot air and steam are then forced through the powdered coal. Some of the coal is burned to provide heat for the process, in which coal and steam combine to produce a gas containing mostly hydrogen, carbon dioxide, nitrogen, and some methane. The Lurgi process produces a low-Btu gas that is burned mostly in power plants to generate electricity. A similar process is used to produce a medium-Btu gas, but in this case pure oxygen is used instead of air.

Gas with a high heat quality—a high-Btu gas—can also be made from coal. This gas, high in methane, is known as substitute natural gas (SNG) and can be used interchangeably with natural gas and distributed through natural gas pipelines.

It is very costly to produce SNG. The process may use hydrogen instead of air, or medium-Btu gas that is produced first, then reacted with hydrogen. Research is currently under way to find methods of bringing the cost down.

This coal gasification pilot plant at Bruceton, Pennsylvania, makes methane gas, which can be substituted for natural gas. Approximately 72 tons of coal are processed there each day.

There is also research and some commercial development (in the Soviet Union) of underground coal gasification, or *in situ* (in place) gasification. In this process, the coal is gasified underground, producing a low-Btu gas. Holes are drilled down to the coal, an oxidizing agent is pumped down through the holes, the coal is ignited, and the combustion products obtained come out through other drilled holes. *See also* IN SITU.

COAL LIQUEFACTION. The process of obtaining a liquid fuel, such as synthetic crude oil (syncrude) or other low-sulfur fuel oil, from coal.

In the 1920s the Fischer-Tropsch process was developed to produce liquid fuel from coal. In this process coal is crushed into a powder, dissolved in solvent oil, heated under pressure, and reacted with hydrogen. The resulting gas is then passed through catalysts—substances that help a chemical reaction to occur but do not themselves enter into the reaction. A liquid fuel is produced.

This expensive process is not widely used today, but interest in coal liquefaction has increased again, due to energy shortages of the 1970s and the rising cost of oil. Two other coal liquefaction processes are now under investigation. In one, called pyrolysis, coal is heated in the absence of air. This produces solids and gases as well as liquids. The amount of liquid, however, is small. In the other process, called coal hydrogenation, hydrogen gas is reacted with coal in the presence of a catalyst to produce liquid fuel. Both processes are expensive, however. Researchers are still trying to come up with a practical and inexpensive way to liquefy coal, particularly in the United States, which has vast supplies of coal but very limited supplies of oil.

COGENERATION. The production of both electric power and heat at the same time. The heat, usually a by-product of the production of energy, can be used to heat buildings or for other purposes.

COKE. A fuel made by heating soft coal in an oven without air. Coke is often used in the smelting of iron ore.

COMBUSTION. Also called burning. A chemical reaction in which certain substances combine rapidly with oxygen. Combustion usually produces heat and light.

COMPRESSOR. A machine for reducing the volume of a gas or other material.

CONDENSATION. The change of a substance from a gas to a liquid. A gas is condensed either by being cooled or by being compressed. For example, when steam, a gas, is cooled, it becomes liquid water.

CONDUCTOR. Any material that carries an electric current and allows that current to flow easily.

CONSERVATION. *See* ENERGY CONSERVATION.

CONTROL ROD. A rod inserted into a nuclear reactor. The purpose of the rod is to absorb neutrons and thereby control the speed of the reaction. *See also* NUCLEAR FISSION and NUCLEAR REACTOR.

COOLING TOWERS. Large towers used for the cooling of water from power plants. Water is a common way to cool a nuclear reactor. This water becomes very hot. It flows through the cooling tower to get rid of the heat. The cooled water can then be pumped back to remove more heat from the reactor core.

A steam generating plant in Kentucky. The cooling towers are on the right. Note the coal, brought in by train, which is used as fuel for the plant.

CORE. The central part of a nuclear reactor. The core is the part of the reactor where nuclear fission takes place. *See also* NUCLEAR FISSION and NUCLEAR REACTOR.

CRITICAL MASS. The smallest amount of nuclear fuel that will support fission as a chain reaction. *See also* NUCLEAR FISSION.

CRUDE OIL. The name given to petroleum as it is pumped from the ground. *See also* PETROLEUM.

Marie Curie, 1867–1934

CURIE, MARIE (1867–1934). The discoverer, with her husband Pierre, of the radioactive elements radium and polonium in 1898. Curie's continuing research into radioactive elements laid the foundation for many later advances in nuclear science. She was awarded two Nobel prizes. Marie Curie was born in Poland but did her scientific work in France.

D

DAM. A barrier placed across a river to stop or control the flow of water. Dams are used in the production of hydroelectric power. *See also* HYDROELECTRIC ENERGY.

The Bonneville lock and dam complex in the northwestern United States

DARRIEUS WIND TURBINE. *See* VERTICAL AXIS WIND TURBINE.

DESTRUCTIVE DISTILLATION. Breaking chemical compounds apart by heat, usually done in the absence of air. The process is also called pyrolysis. *See also* PYROLYSIS.

DEUTERIUM. A type of hydrogen. The nucleus of a deuterium atom contains one neutron and one proton, instead of a single proton as in ordinary hydrogen. Deuterium in the form of heavy water (D_2O) is used as a moderator in nuclear reactors to slow down the fission reaction. Deuterium is also used as a fuel for nuclear fusion. *See also* NUCLEAR FISSION and NUCLEAR FUSION.

DIESEL FUEL. The fuel burned in diesel engines, such as those found in trains, large trucks, and some automobiles. Diesel fuel is made from petroleum but requires less refining than gasoline, the fuel burned in most automobile engines.

DRY CELL. *See* BATTERY.

E

EDISON, THOMAS ALVA (1847–1931). U.S. inventor and one of the most outstanding inventors of all time. Edison's invention of the electric light bulb on October 19, 1879, marked the end of the gaslight era and began the period of widespread use of electricity.

Here, inventor Thomas Alva Edison is doing a radio show.

Edison also invented the phonograph, a moving picture camera, and a type of storage battery. Notable, too, among his many accomplishments was his improvement of the electric generator.

EFFICIENCY. A term that describes how well something works. Energy efficiency refers to the ratio of energy output, or useful work, to the total energy input, or energy consumed.

EINSTEIN, ALBERT (1879–1955). German-born American physicist and one of the greatest theoretical physicists of all time. Einstein is best known for his development of the theories of Special Relativity and General Relativity, showing the relationship between matter and energy. He also contributed to theories on the photoelectric effect, cosmology, and quantum mechanics theory.

Albert Einstein, 1879–1955

He was awarded the Nobel prize in physics in 1921. His work helped make possible the later development of the atomic bomb and commercial nuclear fission and fusion. *See also* NUCLEAR FISSION; NUCLEAR FUSION; and RELATIVITY.

ELECTRICAL ENERGY. Energy resulting from the electric force between charged particles. Electrical energy is one of the most useful types of energy. It is easily produced in power plants and can be transported long distances over wires. In addition, it can be changed into mechanical, heat, light, or sound energy. It is commonly measured in units of kilowatt-hours. *See also* POWER.

ELECTRIC GENERATOR. A device that changes mechanical energy into electrical energy. The generator has a coil of wire that rotates between the poles of a magnet. This produces, or generates, a current of electricity in the coil. In power plants, a fuel is burned, heating water and changing it into steam. The steam spins the blades of a turbine. The turbine rotates the coil in the generator, which creates the electric current. *See also* TURBINE.

ELECTRICITY. The flow of electrons through a conductor. Also called an electric current. Almost any source of energy, such as the fossil fuels, the nucleus of the atom, water, wind, or the sun, can be used to generate electricity. *See also* ELECTRON.

ELECTRODE. In certain electrical devices a terminal through which the electrical current enters or leaves the device. Batteries have two electrodes—the anode, which is the positive terminal, and the cathode, which is the negative terminal. *See also* ANODE; BATTERY; and CATHODE.

ELECTROLYTE. A chemical compound found in batteries. The electrolyte conducts electricity between the electrodes. *See also* BATTERY.

ELECTROMAGNETIC RADIATION. Also called the electromagnetic spectrum. All the various kinds of rays, visible and invisible, produced by the sun and other stars, and emitted, or sent out, in all directions ("radiated") through space. These rays include visible light, which can be seen broken up into its various colors by a prism; infrared rays, which are really rays of heat; ultraviolet rays; radio waves; X rays; and gamma rays.

Radiant energy is usually thought of in terms of waves of light (visible and invisible) of varying lengths. But it can also be thought of as particles carrying energy. These particles are called photons.

ELECTRON. An elementary particle with relatively little mass found orbiting the nucleus of an atom. An electron has a negative charge. When an electron is removed from an atom, it is called a free electron. The flow of electrons along a conductor produces electricity.

ENERGY. The ability to do work, create heat, or produce electricity.

Every living being uses energy all the time. Even when a person is asleep, energy keeps the heart beating and the lungs expanding and contracting. And it is energy that moves cars and planes, sends rockets to outer space, drives factory machines, lights up your home, and keeps buildings warm in cold weather and cool in hot weather.

These professional athletes are clearly using energy in the form in which we most often think of it— the energy of motion.

A rocket uses energy stored in fuel to boost it into space.

Most of the energy on earth comes from the sun. The heat and light of the sun help plants to grow and produce their own food. Humans get energy by eating plants or animals that ate plants. The remains of plants and animals that lived and died millions of years ago make up the coal, oil, and natural gas, called fossil fuels, that we burn for energy. *See also* COAL; FOSSIL FUELS; NATURAL GAS; and PETROLEUM.

The sun's heat causes water to evaporate. When the water vapor turns back into water and falls as rain, rivers flow. The force of flowing water is a source of energy. *See also* HYDROELECTRIC ENERGY.

Early water mills, such as this one from around 1900, were often used to grind grain.

The air in some areas is warmed by the sun more than other areas. The differences in pressure cause air to rush from the cooler to the warmer places, creating wind. The wind is another energy source. *See also* WIND ENERGY.

Many advances in the world were made possible by the development of new sources of energy. Early people used mainly muscle power. Later, people discovered how to use the wind to move their boats. They turned their grain mills either with wind energy or the energy in flowing water. Tamed animals provided the energy to pull plows and wagons and to carry people and goods over long distances. Burning wood was the main source of heat energy for many centuries. By 1900, coal was the main fuel. Now it is oil and natural gas.

The discovery of how to use steam to power machines was an important milestone. Gasoline and electricity became vital sources of energy in recent times. And more recently, nuclear fission came to the fore as an energy source.

This transportable steam engine was built by J.T. Case in 1869.

Energy is made available for use in several ways. One method is chemical change. When some substances combine with oxygen in burning, they give off heat and light. The energy stored in gasoline, released by burning, can be used to power automobiles.

Another path is through physical change. If water is raised to a higher level, it gains potential energy, which is changed into kinetic, or mechanical, energy as it flows down. This, in turn, can be converted into electrical energy. And the electrical energy can be changed into light, heat, or sound energy. Or, it can be turned into radio waves and sent thousands of miles through the air or millions of miles through space. The solar cell changes light energy directly into electricity. *See also* ELECTRICITY; KINETIC ENERGY; MECHANICAL ENERGY; POTENTIAL ENERGY; SOLAR CELL; and SOLAR ENERGY.

The energy found inside the nucleus of the atom is released either when a large nucleus is split (nuclear fission) or when two small nuclei are united (nuclear fusion). Atomic bombs are fission devices. Hydrogen bombs are fission-fusion devices. Nuclear energy can also be controlled for safe electric-power production. *See also* NUCLEAR FISSION and NUCLEAR FUSION.

Alternate sources of energy are our great hope. Nuclear fusion, solar energy, wind and water power, and bioconversion are all renewable sources of energy and may someday end our current energy crisis. *See also* ALTERNATE ENERGY SOURCES and BIOMASS CONVERSION.

ENERGY CONSERVATION. The saving and protecting of energy resources. The main method of energy conservation is using less fuel or electricity.

Until the 1970s, energy was cheap and plentiful. Americans became used to overheated homes, air-conditioned homes and offices, and large cars that consumed great amounts of gasoline. Then, in the mid-1970s, energy became expensive. Eventual shortages of some fuels became apparent.

There are a number of ways to conserve energy. These include programs of education, tax benefits for insulating homes or adding solar-heating systems, research to develop new and better methods of energy production, and the development of energy sources that have not yet been tapped.

In addition, the public needs to change its habits of heating and cooling, to use public transportation instead of private cars whenever possible, to reduce driving speeds to under 55 miles (88 km) per hour, to repair and recycle goods rather than throw them away, to shut off lights, to save water, and generally to use all of nature's resources more carefully and wisely.

ENERGY CONSUMPTION. The amount of energy used. Energy consumption is greatest in electric generating plants, in the various forms of transportation, in home heating and cooling, and in industrial plants, all of which either burn fuels to produce the needed energy or use electrical energy that was obtained by burning fuels.

ENERGY CONVERTERS. Devices to change energy from one form into another.

Energy converters are all around us in today's world. Here are some examples: A gasoline engine changes chemical energy into mechanical energy. An electric light changes electrical energy into light energy. A generator changes mechanical energy into electrical energy. A stove changes chemical energy into heat energy. A doorbell changes electrical energy into mechanical energy and then into sound energy.

ENERGY STORAGE. A system for storing energy for future use. Among the more popular methods of energy storage are electric batteries to store electrical energy, water to store hydroelectric energy, flywheels for storing mechanical energy, and rocks or water for storing heat energy. *See also* BATTERY; FLYWHEEL; HYDROELECTRIC ENERGY; and PUMPED STORAGE.

ENVIRONMENT. All our surroundings, including the land, air, water, and natural resources. The total combined external conditions that affect living organisms, their health and growth.

The human uses of the environment—of the land, water, air, and natural resources of the land—affect all humans and other living organisms as well. Almost all energy decisions have an impact on the environment, and sometimes there is a conflict in deciding what is best in terms of energy availability and price, and what is best in terms of safeguarding the environment. For example, coal is cheap and plentiful, but coal mining can damage the land, and widespread use of high-sulfur coal as a fuel can pollute the air. Nuclear energy causes little air pollution, but it produces radioactive wastes that are hard to dispose of without harming the environment.

EVAPORATION. The changing of a substance from a liquid to a gas or vapor, caused by increasing the speed (energy) at which the molecules are moving.

F

FALLOUT. Airborne particles of radioactive material that fall to earth after a nuclear explosion.

FARADAY, MICHAEL (1791–1867). English chemist and physicist. Faraday worked at the Royal Institution in London for fifty-four years, starting in 1813. In

**Michael Faraday,
1791–1867**

1831, he found that he could produce a current in a coil of copper wire held between the poles of a magnet by either spinning the coil or the magnet. This principle, called electromagnetic induction, is the basis of all electric generators.

Faraday's work led to the discovery of electrons. Faraday was also the first to liquefy many gases. Liquid gases are used today as fuel for some rockets.

Enrico Fermi, 1901–1954

FERMI, ENRICO (1901–1954). American physicist, born in Rome, Italy. Fermi was the first to achieve a sustained nuclear chain reaction. He did so at the University of Chicago on December 2, 1942.

Fermi's atomic research began in 1934 with work on radioactive elements, including those produced by bombardment with neutrons. Without even realizing it, Fermi succeeded in splitting the uranium atom. The process became known as nuclear fission. In 1938, Fermi was awarded the Nobel prize in physics for his breakthrough on nuclear processes. *See also* NUCLEAR FISSION.

FISCHER-TROPSCH PROCESS. *See* COAL LIQUEFACTION.

FISSION. *See* NUCLEAR FISSION.

FLYWHEEL. A heavy wheel used for storing energy. When used in automobiles, the flywheel keeps the engine running smoothly between the firings of each cylinder. The rotating wheel absorbs the extra burst of energy that is released as a cylinder fires. Then the flywheel supplies its energy to the engine until the next cylinder fires.

An experimental bus was tested in Switzerland without an engine, but with a very large, heavy flywheel. Energy drawn from overhead poles every half a mile (0.8 km) powered the wheel, to carry the bus between the poles.

Power plants are also experimenting with flywheels. The wheels are about 15 feet (4.6 m) in diameter and weigh about 150 tons. At times of low electricity demand, the extra current is used to set the wheels spinning at 3,500 revolutions per minute. Each wheel, inside an airtight container, will continue spinning up to a month. At times of peak demand, the flywheel's energy will turn a generator to produce additional electricity.

FOOT-POUND. *See* WORK.

FORCE. The push or pull on a body.

FOSSIL FUELS. Fuels derived from the remains (fossils) of plants or animals that died millions of years ago. They are hydrocarbons, meaning they contain mostly hydrogen and carbon. Coal, oil, and natural gas are fossil fuels.

When most plants and animals die, they decay and are decomposed by bacteria. A small number, though, are buried under layers of earth, water, rock, or other plants. These plants and animals do not decay in the same way as remains left exposed to the air. The heat and pressure eventually turn their remains into coal, petroleum, and natural gas—the fossil fuels. *See also* CARBONIFEROUS PERIOD; COAL; HYDROCARBON; NATURAL GAS; and PETROLEUM.

FUEL. Any substance that can be burned to produce heat. The material used for fission in a nuclear reactor is also called a fuel.

FUEL CELL. A device that produces electrical energy directly from chemical energy. The first fuel cell was made in 1839 by William Grove. But the first practical ones were developed in the late 1950s for use in the *Gemini* and *Apollo* spacecraft.

The principle of the fuel cell is simple. There are two porous plates (plates with holes) separated by a liquid that conducts electricity. In a typical fuel cell, hydrogen gas is passed through one plate, and oxygen is passed through the other. The hydrogen and oxygen react to create an electrical current that flows between the two plates. This current can be wired into an electrical circuit. At the same time, the fuel cell produces water and some heat.

Fuel cells do not add to pollution. They are silent, do not need to be cooled, and are efficient. Most electrical generation, which uses steam to drive a generator, is about 40 percent efficient. Fuel cells do much better. They reach efficiencies of up to 70 percent.

FUSION. *See* NUCLEAR FUSION.

GAMMA RAYS. Deadly high-energy radiation of a short wavelength. Gamma rays, which are very penetrating, are released during nuclear fission. The sun, which emits energy by the process of nuclear fusion, also sends out gamma rays, but these do not normally penetrate the earth's atmosphere. Gamma rays produced by nuclear fission on earth can be blocked by a shield of thick lead.

GASIFICATION. Changing a substance such as coal into a gas. *See also* COAL GASIFICATION.

GASOHOL. An automobile fuel made of gasoline and alcohol. The alcohol is made from fermentation of plant products. Gasohol usually contains 90 percent gasoline and 10 percent alcohol. *See also* BIOMASS CONVERSION.

GASOLINE. A fuel obtained from crude oil, or petroleum, used mainly in internal combustion engines, such as in automobiles. Gasoline is made by heating crude oil in a refining process. The gasoline part of the crude oil comes off as a vapor. The vapor is then cooled into a liquid. It is further refined and certain additives are put in to produce the gasoline that is used in cars and trucks.

GENERATOR. *See* ELECTRIC GENERATOR.

GEOTHERMAL ENERGY. Energy that comes from the natural heat of the earth. The rocks beneath the surface, in some areas of the world, are very hot. Scientists believe that these rocks contain large amounts of the radioactive elements thorium and uranium.

As these radioactive elements have decayed, they have heated up the surrounding rocks. The heat is trapped, and over millions of years it has built up to its present high levels. This is the main source of geothermal energy.

Geothermal energy usually takes one of three forms. The most useful is the dry steam that forms from the water that is trapped in the heated rocks. The steam forces its way to the surface, where it is sent through pipes to drive the generators of a power plant to produce electricity.

More common than geothermal steam are giant underground pools of hot water mixed with steam. Deep wells must be dug to get the water out. The steam can then be used to generate electricity. The hot water can be used for many purposes, such as home heating, agriculture, and industry. One industrial use of the hot water is to produce electricity by vaporizing a low-boiling-point fluid to drive a generator. These direct uses are simple, except for the problem of minerals in the water, which can clog pipes and corrode metal equipment.

Hot rocks that are very close to the surface are a promising energy source. Engineers drill twin holes down to the hot rock. They pump water down through one hole. The water is heated by the hot rock and comes up through the other hole, either as superheated water or steam. More research is needed before this energy source can become practical for use, however.

The largest geothermal energy source in use is the dry steam field called The Geysers in northern California. It supplies the electrical needs for a city of 500,000 people. Reykjavik, Iceland, with a population of 100,000, gets most of its heat and warm water from geothermal wells. Some government experts believe there is enough geothermal energy beneath the United States to provide several times the energy needed by our country every year.

GEYSER. A natural hot spring that ejects hot water and steam into the air. The geyser comes from the thermal energy at relatively shallow depths beneath the earth's surface. The most famous geyser in the United States is called Old Faithful; it is located in Yellowstone National Park in Wyoming. *See also* GEOTHERMAL ENERGY.

GREENHOUSE EFFECT. The buildup of carbon dioxide in the air that allows the sun's rays to heat the earth's surface, but does not let the heat escape. This gradually raises the earth's temperature. Since this is similar to what happens in a greenhouse, it is called the greenhouse effect.

Some scientists fear that the extensive burning of hydrocarbons has drastically increased the amount of carbon dioxide in the air and may be causing a greenhouse effect on earth, the results of which could be disastrous. For example, warmer temperatures over an extended period of time could melt the polar icecaps, causing the flooding of coastal cities.

HALF-LIFE. The time it takes for half the atoms of a radioactive substance to disintegrate, or decay. The half-life of a substance can range anywhere from a millionth of a second to billions of years.

HEAT. A form of energy that flows from one object to another because of the temperature difference between them. Heat is usually measured in Btus. *See also* BTU and CALORIE.

HEAT ENERGY. Energy produced by the rapid shaking back and forth, or vibrating, of tiny particles of matter called molecules. Heating water, for instance, causes the molecules of water to vibrate much more violently than they do in cooler water.

HEAT EXCHANGER. A device for transferring heat from one entity or medium to another. In the most common type of heat exchanger, heat is transferred from one fluid (liquid or gas) to another through a solid, usually a metal of high heat conductivity. One type of heat exchanger, widely used in Scandinavian countries, where houses are tightly sealed against the cold, pulls fresh air inside and passes stagnant air to the outside through ducts separated by a wall that allows the cool, clean air to absorb the heat of the stagnant air on its way out. This system not only transfers heat but also provides clean air, reducing the possibility of indoor air pollution.

HEAT PUMP. A device that efficiently heats or cools a room by transferring or pumping warm air from one area to another to either heat or cool the room involved. A heat pump is more efficient than an electric heater, and it is gaining in popularity in certain geographical areas, particularly in relatively mild climates.

HEATING VALUE. The amount of heat energy that can be obtained from a fuel. Heating value is often measured as Btus per cubic foot (28.3 cu cm) or as calories. *See also* BTU and CALORIE.

HEAVY WATER. Water that contains a high proportion of heavy-hydrogen, or deuterium, atoms to ordinary hydrogen atoms. Heavy water is used in some nuclear reactors because it slows down the nuclear reactions. *See also* DEUTERIUM.

HELIOSTAT. A mirror on a movable frame that turns to reflect or focus the

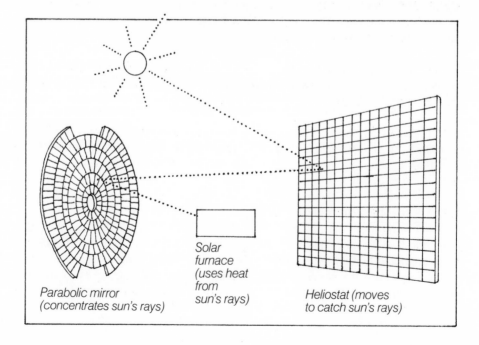

Parabolic mirror (concentrates sun's rays)

Solar furnace (uses heat from sun's rays)

Heliostat (moves to catch sun's rays)

Sixty-three separate heliostats make up this giant solar furnace located in southern France.

sun's rays onto a solar collector. *See also* SOLAR COLLECTOR and SOLAR ENERGY.

HELMONT, JAN BAPTISTA VAN (1577–1664). The first person to make gas from coal. Helmont was an alchemist in Brussels, Belgium, who was trying to produce gold out of other materials. In one experiment, in 1609, as he was heating coal, he found that a gas was produced. When he discovered that the gas could burn, he named it "ghost." The word *gas* is believed to have come from the Dutch word for ghost, which is *geest*.

HORSEPOWER. A measure of power. *See* POWER.

HOT SPRING. A natural spring whose water temperature is higher than the atmospheric temperature.

HYDROCARBON. Any organic compound made up chiefly of carbon and hydrogen atoms. Those with only a few atoms in each molecule are usually gases. Those with more atoms are commonly liquid. And those with the largest number of atoms are mostly solid. The fossil fuels are hydrocarbons. *See also* FOSSIL FUELS.

HYDROELECTRIC ENERGY. Electricity produced by using flowing or falling water. The typical arrangement is to have water pass through the spillway of a dam in order to drive a turbine and generator. Sometimes the water going down a waterfall is used to spin the turbine blades.

This dam on the Clinch River in eastern Tennessee can produce over 100,000 kilowatts of energy at any one time.

HYDROGEN. The lightest element. Ordinary hydrogen has one proton and no neutrons in its nucleus. Two important isotopes, or varieties, of hydrogen are deuterium, with one proton and one neutron in the nucleus, and tritium, with one proton and two neutrons. *See also* DEUTERIUM and TRITIUM.

**The explosion
of a
hydrogen bomb**

HYDROGEN BOMB. An explosive device, first tested in 1952, that is the most powerful of all weapons of warfare. The hydrogen bomb, or H-bomb, as it is called, is based on very rapid nuclear fusion. The nuclei of atoms of hydrogen are joined, or fused, together to form helium nuclei, with the consequent release of energy. Slower, controlled nuclear fusion is now being studied as an important source of energy for the future. *See also* NUCLEAR FUSION.

IN SITU. Latin words meaning "in place." The expression is sometimes used to describe processing a fossil fuel while it is still in the ground. Two examples of *in situ* processing are removing oil from oil shale underground and changing coal into gas without mining the coal. *See also* COAL GASIFICATION and OIL SHALE.

INERTIAL CONFINEMENT. One method of containing the plasma (very hot gas) used in nuclear fusion. The other major method is known as magnetic confinement.

In inertial confinement, the plasma is bombarded from all sides by a powerful energy source, such as from several laser beams. This creates enough heat and pressure to start the fusion reaction.

The best-known piece of inertial confinement equipment was the Shiva Target Chamber at the Lawrence Livermore National Laboratory in California. It was named for the many-armed Hindu god of love and destruction. In Shiva, twenty separate laser beams were aimed at the fuel, delivering a flash of 20 billion kilowatts for a billionth of a second. Shiva has been dismantled, but a new confinement vessel, Nova, is now under construction at Livermore. *See also* MAGNETIC CONFINEMENT; NUCLEAR FUSION; and PLASMA.

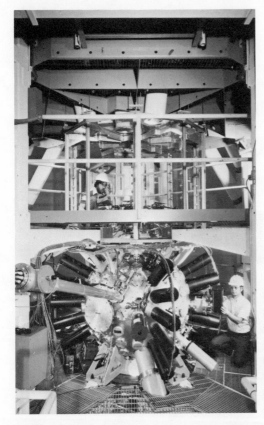

Researchers at Lawrence Livermore Laboratory prepare the Shiva target chamber for a fusion experiment. Shiva's lasers will focus 30 trillion watts of optical power on the tiny fusion target in the center of the chamber.

INSULATION. A material that prevents the transfer of heat. Usually refers to layers of a porous material that can trap air and stop heat from leaving. Also called thermal insulation.

ION. An atom with either a positive or negative electrical charge. Ions are created by removing electrons from or adding them to the atom, which is normally electrically neutral.

ISOTOPES. Atoms of the same chemical element that have different masses. The difference in mass is caused by different numbers of neutrons in the nuclei of the atoms. *See also* ATOM.

J-K

JOULE. A metric unit of work or energy. *See also* WORK.

KEROGEN. The solid material found in oil shale that, when heated, becomes oil. *See also* OIL SHALE.

KEROSENE. One of the products made from crude oil by the refining process. *See also* REFINERY.

KILOWATT. Equal to 1,000 watts. *See also* POWER.

KINETIC ENERGY. The energy of motion. Among the many kinds of kinetic energy is the energy from flowing water.

L

LASER. A device for producing a powerful, sharply focused beam of light. The light of a laser is coherent, differing from ordinary light in that it is made up of waves of all the same wavelength. Laser beams are used in some approaches to nuclear fusion and in many applications in industry and medicine. The term *laser* is really an acronym for *L*ight *A*mplification by *S*timulated *E*mission of *R*adiation. *See also* INERTIAL CONFINEMENT and NUCLEAR FUSION.

LIGHT ENERGY. A form of electromagnetic energy from the sun that can pass through empty space. Light energy travels out from a source at a speed of about 186,000 miles (300,000 km) per second.

LIGHT-WATER REACTOR. A nuclear reactor in which the coolant surrounding the core is ordinary water. It is called a light-water reactor to distinguish it from reactors that use what is known as heavy water—water containing deuterium atoms— and reactors that cool the core using a gas. *See also* DEUTERIUM; HEAVY WATER; and NUCLEAR REACTOR.

LIQUEFACTION. The process of changing a solid substance to a liquid. *See also* COAL LIQUEFACTION.

LIQUEFIED NATURAL GAS. Natural gas that has been changed from a gas into a liquid. The natural gas is compressed and cooled to −260°F (−160°C). It becomes a liquid and shrinks to about 1/600 of its original volume. This makes it easier and more economical to store and transport.

LNG, as it is called, is transported in tanker ships that keep it cold and under pressure, for reasons of safety. When the pressure is removed, the LNG becomes a gas again. It can then be pumped through the same pipelines that are used for ordinary natural gas.

LIQUID METAL FAST BREEDER REACTOR. A breeder reactor in which the coolant is the metal sodium in a liquid state. *See also* BREEDER REACTOR.

LURGI PROCESS. A coal gasification process. The Lurgi process is used commercially in America and in Europe and is the basis of many new processes being tested and developed. *See also* COAL GASIFICATION.

M

MAGNETIC CONFINEMENT. A system used to contain the plasma in nuclear fusion. It is also called a magnetic bottle. The other method of nuclei confinement is known as inertial confinement.

The Princeton fusion device

Powerful magnets confine the plasma in this experimental fusion device located at Lawrence Livermore Laboratory.

One magnetic field device is the Tokamak, which is in the shape of a giant doughnut. Powerful magnetic fields hold the plasma in place. The best known Tokamak is being tested at Princeton University.

A second type is the magnetic mirror. Here the magnetic field operates at both ends of a tube, reflecting the nuclei back and forth within the tube. The most famous magnetic mirror is at the Lawrence Livermore National Laboratory at the University of California.

Theta magnetic pinch devices are still another approach to magnetic confinement. They keep the nuclei in a straight tube similar to the one used in the magnetic mirrors. The most successful theta magnetic pinch device is at Los Alamos Laboratory in New Mexico. *See also* INERTIAL CONFINEMENT; NUCLEAR FUSION; and PLASMA.

MAGNETOHYDRODYNAMIC GENERATOR (MHD). A type of generator that produces electricity directly from fuels. The fuels are burned to produce very hot gases at temperatures as high as 5,000°F (2,760°C). When these gases are passed through a magnetic field, there is a flow of electricity in electrodes set in the field. MHD power plants produce electricity with little pollution and up to 60 percent efficiency. This is much better than ordinary electric power plants, which are only 40 percent efficient.

MECHANICAL ENERGY. The movement of objects. Flowing water, blowing wind, a tight spring unwinding, a falling weight—all these are examples of mechanical energy.

MELTDOWN. *See* NUCLEAR FISSION.

METHANE. The main part of natural gas. Methane is colorless, odorless, and burns easily. It is formed by the decay of organic matter. The chemical formula for methane is CH_4—one carbon atom and four hydrogen atoms.

MICROWAVES. Very short radio waves. Microwaves are used for long-distance transmission of electrical signals and in home electronic ovens, among

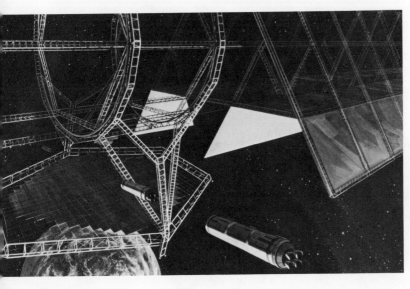

A solar power satellite system, such as this one depicted by a NASA artist, would utilize microwaves for the transmission of electricity.

other uses. It is thought they might be used for the transmission of solar energy from solar power satellites in space. *See also* SOLAR CELL and SOLAR POWER SATELLITE.

MOLECULE. The smallest unit of a substance made up of two or more atoms. The atoms can be the same or different. All substances are made up of molecules. Each molecule of a substance contains the same number and kinds of atoms. A molecule of the compound water, for example, always contains two hydrogen atoms and one oxygen atom (H_2O). *See also* ATOM.

NATURAL GAS. A gas found naturally in rock formations beneath the surface of the earth, near deposits of oil. Natural gas is second only to crude oil in importance as a fuel. It is made up of the gases methane, ethane, propane, butane, pentane, and hexane. Natural gas contains about 1,032 Btus per cubic foot (28.3 cu cm).

Natural gas was formed under the ground from the remains of tiny plants and animals that lived millions of years ago in swamps or near water. The matter from these plants and animals made a thick layer of ooze, which was covered by earth and rock. Under the heat and pressure of the earth, the decaying matter slowly changed into oil and gas. The deposits collected in giant sealed pools. These pools are tapped to release the gas, which comes roaring out because of the great pressure. Sometimes the temperature of the gas is as high as 392°F (200°C) when it reaches the surface.

For a long time natural gas was considered a waste material of no value. To get rid of it, the early oil drillers burned, or flared, the gas at the mouth of the oil well. Since the value of natural gas has become known, none is wasted.

About twenty states in the United States have sizable amounts of natural gas. Two states, Texas and Louisiana, produce nearly 70 percent the total output of the United States.

NEUTRON. A particle found within the nucleus of most atoms. The neutron has no electrical charge. But it has about the same mass as a proton, the other nuclear particle. Neutrons are used to sustain the chain reaction in nuclear fission. *See also* NUCLEAR FISSION.

NUCLEAR ENERGY. Also called nuclear power. Involves the use of reactions in the nucleus of the atom to generate power. There are two types of nuclear reactions—fission and fusion. *See also* NUCLEAR FISSION and NUCLEAR FUSION.

NUCLEAR FISSION. A nuclear reaction in which heavy atoms are split apart, releasing large amounts of energy. This process occurs with great speed in an atom bomb. It occurs much more slowly and under controlled conditions in a nuclear reactor.

    An isotope (variety) of uranium is the fuel usually used for the creation of nuclear energy through fission. This radioactive ore has a densely packed nucleus and tends to be unstable, that is, it tends to emit particles such as neutrons on its own, until it changes into a more stable element.

The world's first nuclear reactor, depicted here, was assembled at the University of Chicago. On December 2, 1942, a group of scientists, led by Enrico Fermi, achieved the first self-sustaining fission chain reaction.

Inspectors check the fuel rods, containing enriched uranium fuel pellets, that will be placed inside a nuclear reactor.

Before the uranium can be used, it must be refined and enriched. When it is ready, it is put inside the reactor core, or target chamber. Then a neutron, which is an atomic particle found inside the nucleus of an atom, is aimed at the uranium and fired. This neutron is absorbed by the nucleus of the uranium atom, making that atom even heavier and more unstable and causing it to split and release some of the neutrons within its own nucleus. Those neutrons bombard the nucleus of another uranium atom, causing the second atom to break apart and release more neutrons. These neutrons then strike other atoms of uranium, splitting these atoms and releasing more neutrons. And so the process goes on, without stop and without further outside intervention. This process is called a chain reaction.

Each time an atom splits, there is a release of energy—the energy that held the nucleus together in the first place. If this energy, in the form of heat, is released all at once, there is a great explosion. This is how the atom bomb works. But if the reaction is slowed by the use of control rods, the heat becomes a usable source of energy. It can be put to work heating water to produce steam that can then turn a turbine and generate electricity.

About 13 percent of the energy generated in the United States today is produced by the process of nuclear fission. Producing energy by nuclear fission has several advantages when compared with the burning of fossil fuels for electricity. No pollutants such as smoke are added to the air. There is a greater supply of uranium available than of fossil fuels, particularly oil. Breeder reactors actually produce more nuclear material than they use. And the fuel costs, in the long run, are lower for uranium than for other fuels.

Nuclear fission does have a number of problems, though. There is the danger of radioactivity. Radioactivity is the sending out of invisible particles and rays from the nucleus of the atom. Some of these particles and rays are very harmful to most living things. Gamma rays in particular, which can penetrate most solid objects, are extremely deadly. A thick wall of lead must be built around the reactor to contain them.

In the course of their operation, nuclear power plants also produce waste products, called radwaste, that are radioactive and deadly. These wastes remain radioactive for thousands or even millions of years. Most have been temporarily sealed inside large steel drums, but a more permanent and safe way of disposing of them must be found. Burying them deep inside old salt mines, where the danger of leakage is small, appears to be the most favored solution at present. Test mines are scheduled to be built starting in 1986.

Another radwaste danger occurs in transporting it through populated areas. It is conceivable that some radiation could leak out of the temporary containers while they are on their way to permanent storage.

Some nuclear power plants use water from nearby lakes or rivers to cool the reactors, thereby raising the temperature of these bodies of water. This may be harmful to plant and animal life living in those waters.

In recent years, public concern and the delays and increased cost of installing safer plants have slowed down and in some cases completely stopped the construction of new nuclear power plants. Occasional reports of leakages of radiation from existing plants have alarmed nearby residents. An accident that occurred in March 1979 at the Three Mile Island (TMI) nuclear power plant, located near Harrisburg, Pennsylvania, alerted the public to another danger.

The danger of a runaway chain reaction during fission energy production must always be guarded against. In the control room of a nuclear power plant, operators are on duty at all times to see that everything is running smoothly.

Though the explosion of a nuclear power plant is not possible (the uranium is not enriched enough to allow it to explode), the core of the reactor does get very hot, and if not properly cooled can cause a runaway chain reaction. This, in turn, can cause what is popularly known as a meltdown, which means that the core becomes so hot that it melts through the concrete containment building and sinks into the ground. This can cause dangerous contamination of underground water and other serious problems. Disaster was averted at TMI, but the incident so alarmed the public that the nuclear energy industry suffered severe setbacks in its growth afterward.

See also BREEDER REACTOR; CORE; GAMMA RAYS; and LIGHT-WATER REACTOR.

NUCLEAR FUSION. A nuclear reaction that unites, or fuses, two small atomic nuclei to produce one larger nucleus. The reaction also releases a great amount of energy. Since fusion occurs only at very high temperatures, it is also called a thermonuclear reaction.

The sun is the earth's main source of energy. It produces its energy through nuclear fusion. This process takes place at the center of the sun. Here the temperature is measured in millions of degrees. It is hot enough to ionize (remove electrons from) the hydrogen atoms inside the sun, producing a plasma (very hot gas) consisting of negatively charged free electrons and positively charged ions. The ions collide with each other with enough force to overcome the repellent force of the positive charges (like charges usually repel each other). These ions then fuse to form new nuclei, releasing energy in the process.

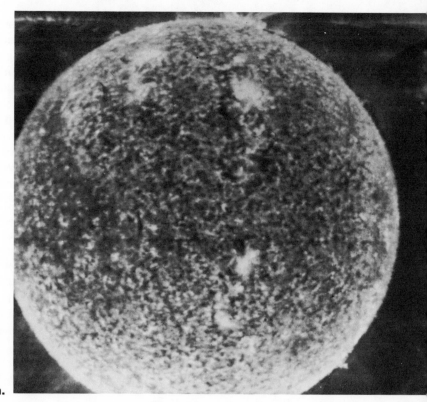

Ultimately, almost all energy on earth comes from the sun.

On earth, nuclear fusion is usually accomplished by combining two isotopes (varieties) of hydrogen. The nuclei of deuterium, which contain one proton and one neutron, are fused with the nuclei of tritium, which contain one proton and two neutrons. (An ordinary hydrogen nucleus contains only a proton, no neutrons.)

When the nuclei of deuterium and tritium fuse, the result is helium. The helium nucleus contains two protons and two neutrons. A neutron is emitted during the reaction and energy is released. The amount of energy produced by the fusion reaction is even greater than that obtained by splitting an atom, or nuclear fission.

In order for fusion to occur, the atoms have to be heated to around 180 million degrees F (100 million degrees C), creating a special state of matter known as plasma. Also, the plasma has to be held, or confined, long enough for fusion to occur. No practical or commercial way to sustain nuclear fusion, so it can produce more energy than it consumes, has yet been found.

Two basic approaches to plasma containment are now being tried. In magnetic confinement, powerful magnetic fields contain the plasma while the reaction takes place. The main designs are the Tokamak (a torus, or doughnut-shaped container) and magnetic mirrors. The other approach is known as inertial confinement. This method uses a number of powerful laser beams to hold the plasma and raise it to the necessary temperatures.

Thus far, nuclear fusion for the generation of useful energy exists only in the laboratory. Yet many scientists believe fusion will become the major energy source of the future. Supplies of oil and natural gas are running out. Coal causes pollution. We may not be able to produce large enough amounts of hydroelectric, wind, or solar energy to fill the need. And nuclear fission can be dangerous.

The advantages of nuclear fusion seem clear. The deuterium and tritium come from ocean water and are in great supply. The fusion reaction is relatively clean, although tritium shows some slight radioactivity. But, as pointed out earlier, research is still needed to come up with a practical fusion device that can be used for commercial power production. *See also* INERTIAL CONFINEMENT; MAGNETIC CONFINEMENT; and PLASMA.

NUCLEAR POWER PLANT. A plant for generating electrical power by using a nuclear reactor instead of burning a fossil fuel as the source of heat.

NUCLEAR REACTOR. A device that allows nuclear fission to take place under controlled conditions.

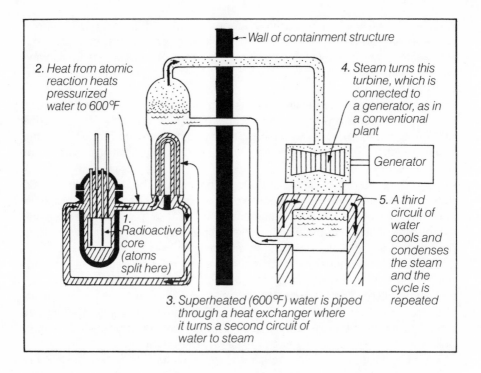

2. Heat from atomic reaction heats pressurized water to 600°F

← Wall of containment structure

4. Steam turns this turbine, which is connected to a generator, as in a conventional plant

Generator

1. Radioactive core (atoms split here)

5. A third circuit of water cools and condenses the steam and the cycle is repeated

3. Superheated (600°F) water is piped through a heat exchanger where it turns a second circuit of water to steam

The nuclear reactor core contains pellets of uranium set in long rods. During fission, the nuclei of the uranium atoms are split, releasing great amounts of energy.

Also in the reactor are control rods. These contain material that absorbs some of the neutrons released by the fission, thereby controlling the speed of the reaction.

Nuclear reactors become very hot because of the energy released by the fission. To prevent any damage from occurring, the core is usually cooled by either water or another liquid. In some nuclear power plants the water heated by the reactor is changed directly to steam. This steam drives a generator to produce electricity. In others, a different liquid is heated by the reactor. This hot liquid is then piped through water, changing the water to steam for electricity production. There are also reactors, called breeder reactors, which produce more nuclear fuel than they use up. *See also* BREEDER REACTOR and NUCLEAR FISSION.

NUCLEAR REGULATORY COMMISSION (NRC). The agency of the federal government responsible for the safety of the nation's nuclear power plants and for regulating the peaceful uses of nuclear energy.

NUCLEAR WASTE. Also called radwaste. Material left over after fission has taken place within the reactor of a nuclear power plant. The material remains radioactive for thousands or millions of years. It must be stored to prevent living things from being exposed to the radioactivity. Nuclear wastes are usually sealed in containers and buried. *See also* NUCLEAR FISSION and RADIOACTIVITY.

NUCLEUS. The central core of all atoms. Inside the nucleus are the protons and neutrons, held together by what are known as the weak and strong nuclear forces. Circling the nucleus are the electrons. The plural of nucleus is nuclei. *See also* ATOM.

OCEAN THERMAL ENERGY. A source of energy based on the natural heating of the surface of ocean waters by the sun. Surface water in the world's tropical areas is about 77°F (25°C) all year long. The water at a depth of 1,000 feet (300 m) is about 41°F (5°C). This difference in temperature is called the ocean thermal gradient. The ocean thermal process used for energy production is called Ocean Thermal Energy Conversion, or OTEC.

First, a long vertical tube or cylinder is placed in the water. Warm water enters at the top and heats a cylinder that contains a liquid with a low boiling point. This changes the liquid to a gas.

The gas drives a turbine, which drives a generator to produce electricity. Then the gas is cooled by the cold, deeper ocean water flowing around the bottom of the cylinder. This returns the gas to the liquid state. The cycle then starts again—liquid heated to gas, gas cooled back to liquid, and so on.

Scientists have the know-how to produce ocean thermal energy. But there are still some problems. Tropical waters are not usually near large centers of population, so there is the expense of transporting the electricity. Also, it is difficult to make the power plants seaworthy and to protect them from sealife. And lastly, the cost is still too high to compete with the more traditional sources of electricity. Research is seeking solutions to these problems.

OCEAN THERMAL GRADIENT. The difference in temperature between surface waters warmed by the sun and the deeper, cooler waters. It is used for ocean thermal energy production. *See* also OCEAN THERMAL ENERGY.

OIL. *See* PETROLEUM.

OIL SHALE. A type of rock that contains oil. The technical name is laminated marlstone. Locked inside the oil shale is a solid substance called kerogen. Kerogen is really oil that has not been fully formed because of heat and pressure conditions.

Oil is produced from oil shale by heating it to temperatures of approximately 1,000°F (538°C). This drives the kerogen out as a gas. When the gas is cooled, it becomes a liquid similar to the crude oil that comes from oil wells.

The oil can be removed from the shale either above the ground or under the ground. Either the shale is mined, brought to the surface, and heated to get out the kerogen, or it is heated in place underground, called *in situ*. In the second case, just the oil is pumped up.

It is presently very expensive to produce oil from oil shale. There is the problem of getting rid of the leftover rock after the oil is removed. Great amounts of energy are required to heat the shale. Processing the shale also uses lots of water. Yet there is little water available in the areas where most of the large deposits of oil shale are found. And the process gives off some gases that can pollute the air.

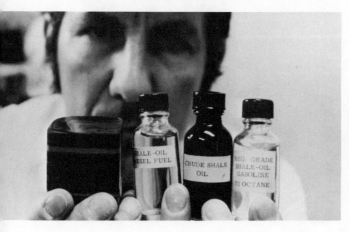

Shale, which is a kind of rock, yields several different liquids that can be burned as fuel to fulfill energy needs. But removing oil from the rock is a costly and environmentally risky procedure.

Oil shale processing may become important to America. The United States Department of Interior estimates that there are at least 2 trillion barrels (318 trillion liters) of oil shale in the Green River area of Colorado, Utah, and Wyoming. Eighty billion barrels (12,700 billion liters) of oil could be recovered using today's methods. This is more than the oil reserve of Saudi Arabia, the largest oil-producer in the world. And it is nearly twenty times more than the crude oil reserves in the United States. At present rates of use, the shale oil could fill U.S. energy needs for about a hundred years. However, the serious problems of rock removal, heat use, water availability, and high production costs must be solved before large-scale commercial production could begin.

OIL WELL. A hole drilled into the earth to search for oil and bring it up to the surface.

When a company decides to drill, a derrick, or large platform, is set up above the spot chosen. A large bit, usually made of sharp steel, cuts into the ground and drills the well to the level of the oil. Oil well workers, called roughnecks, oversee the installation of the equipment and the smooth operation of the well.

This offshore drilling platform stands in Alaska's Cook Inlet. Some of the newer rigs can drill for oil in water more than 1,000 feet (300 m) deep.

OILFIELD. An area over a large pool or pools of oil. Usually refers to an area that has already been or can easily be put into production.

OPEC. Acronym for *O*rganization of *P*etroleum *E*xporting *C*ountries. OPEC is a group of oil-producing nations that joined together in 1960 to coordinate the prices and production of petroleum by member nations, who control most of the world's petroleum. These countries include Abu Dhabi, Algeria, Indonesia, Iran, Iraq, Kuwait, Libya, Nigeria, Qatar, Saudi Arabia, and Venezuela.

OTEC. Acronym for *O*cean *T*hermal *E*nergy *C*onversion. *See also* OCEAN THERMAL ENERGY.

PASSIVE SOLAR ENERGY SYSTEM. A system that uses natural, or structural, parts of a building to collect and store solar energy for heating or cooling. The system needs no moving parts, such as pumps or fans, to distribute the solar heat.

One type of passive system is called a direct gain system. This uses large south-facing windows in a house or building to admit the sun's rays. Concrete or other dense materials are used in the floors or walls to store the heat from the sun. This heat is then given off slowly to maintain a comfortable temperature in the room.

Another type of system is a south-facing wall that is made of concrete or containers filled with water. The outside of the wall is covered with plastic or glass to admit the sun's rays. The concrete or container is painted black to absorb the energy from the sun. The heat is then slowly given off to the rooms. This system is called a thermal storage wall.

A third type of passive system consists of a greenhouse attached to the south side of a house. A thermal storage wall may be located between the greenhouse and the house itself. Solar heat collected in the greenhouse is allowed to pass into the house through openings in the wall. Some of the heat is stored in the wall. *See also* ACTIVE SOLAR ENERGY SYSTEM; SOLAR COLLECTOR; SOLAR ENERGY; SOLAR ENERGY SYSTEM; SOLAR HOUSE.

PEAK POWER LOAD. The time of greatest electric power demand. The summer peak time is usually early afternoon. In winter, peak time is generally late afternoon.

PEAT. Decayed vegetable matter in the soil that can be burned as a fuel. Over long periods of time and under the right conditions, peat becomes coal. *See also* COAL.

PETROCHEMICAL. Any chemical made from petroleum. Among the more important products made from petrochemicals are plastics, drugs, synthetic fibers, paints, fertilizers, and detergents. *See also* PETROLEUM and REFINERY.

PETROLEUM. A dark liquid that forms naturally in the upper levels of the earth; also called oil.

Petroleum is mainly made up of hydrocarbons. Hydrocarbons are compounds of carbon and hydrogen atoms, but may also contain sulfur, oxygen, and nitrogen. A number of very important and useful products are made from petroleum. These include gasoline, fuel oil, lubricants, kerosene, and asphalt. In addition, there are the petrochemicals, from which products such as plastics, drugs, detergents, and fertilizers are produced.

Petroleum was formed millions of years ago in the oceans and swamps that covered the earth during prehistoric times. When the tiny plants and animals that lived in and around the water died, their remains fell to the muddy bottoms. Sand and mud fell on top. The weight formed them into layers. Then, over millions of years, heat, pressure, bacterial action, and perhaps other natural processes changed the remains into petroleum and natural gas. In time, huge pools of petroleum formed below the surface of the earth.

Scientists study rock formations and gravity and magnetism readings to try to locate the underground petroleum. They drill wells in likely places. When they make a strike, the oil either flows up, because of pressure in the pool of oil, or it is pumped up.

From the oilfield, the petroleum is taken to a refinery. Here the crude oil is separated into many different compounds by heating. Heating changes parts of the petroleum into a mixture of various gases. These gases are then separated and cooled to get a variety of substances. The oil is treated in other ways to make specific products and to remove unwanted impurities. From the refinery, the various petroleum products go to storage and then to the users.

PHOTOSYNTHESIS. The process of growth in green plants. During photosynthesis, the plants combine the energy from sunlight with water and carbon dioxide to make food. Some of the light energy is stored in the plant as chemical energy. Human beings get this energy by eating plants, or by eating animals that eat plants. We can also release this energy by burning the plants or by allowing them to decay. *See also* BIOMASS CONVERSION and FOSSIL FUELS.

PHOTOVOLTAIC CELL. A device that converts light, particularly sunlight, into electricity. The more popular name is solar cell. *See also* SOLAR CELL.

PIPELINE. A series of connected pipes built to carry a product, such as oil, over a long distance.

A pipeline is often used to transport natural gas.

PLASMA. Gas at a temperature above 10,000°F (5,500°C). The atomic nuclei used in nuclear fusion are in the form of a plasma. Plasma contains both positive and negative ions. This makes it electrically neutral. Since it behaves differently from solids, liquids, and gases, plasma is sometimes called the "fourth state of matter." *See also* NUCLEAR FUSION.

PLUTONIUM. A radioactive element that can be used as a fuel in nuclear reactors. Plutonium can be produced in a breeder reactor. *See also* BREEDER REACTOR.

POLLUTION. Adding various harmful or poisonous substances to the earth's air, land, or water that do not belong there. Pollution of the air results from cars and trucks burning gasoline, from factories releasing gases and particulates, and from the burning of heating oil and waste products. Pollution of the land comes from garbage or dangerous chemical wastes thrown in dumps. Water pollution is caused by sewage being dumped into oceans, lakes, or rivers, spills of oil or other chemicals, and factories releasing hot water or chemical wastes into bodies of water.

POTENTIAL ENERGY. Stored up energy. Water high up on a mountain has potential energy, which is released as the water flows down the mountain.

POWER. The rate at which work is done or energy expended. Power is equal to work divided by time. It can be measured in three main ways. One is in foot-pounds per second. Another is in watts, which are joules divided by seconds. And the final way is by horsepower. One horsepower equals 550 foot-pounds per second, or 746 watts. *See also* WORK.

POWER PLANT. A facility for producing electric power. In fossil fuel power plants either coal, oil, or natural gas is burned to heat water, changing the water into steam. The steam then drives a turbine, which spins a generator, thus producing the electricity. In nuclear power plants the source of heat is a nuclear reactor instead of a fossil fuel.

PRESSURIZED WATER REACTOR. A common type of nuclear reactor used in electric power production. The core of the reactor heats water in a high-pressure system. This water is then piped through a boiler. In the boiler it heats other water to make steam before returning to the reactor. The steam then drives a turbine to generate electricity.

PROTON. A particle found within the nucleus of all atoms. A proton has a positive electrical charge.

PUMPED STORAGE. An energy storage system used in hydroelectric power production. During periods of little demand for electricity, energy is used to pump water up to a storage reservoir at a higher level. When the demand for electricity is high, the water is allowed to flow downhill. As it flows down it drives turbines, generating electricity. *See also* HYDROELECTRIC ENERGY.

PYROLYSIS. Heating a substance in the absence of oxygen. Pyrolysis is used to change coal to synthetic gas and oil. The process leaves an ash, called char, behind. It is also used to change organic wastes into fuel products. Pyrolysis is also called destructive distillation.

R

RADIATION. The emission of particles and waves through space or matter. These particles and waves are given off by a source, such as a star (our sun is a star) and carry varying levels of energy. Heat, light, radio waves, and X rays are all forms of radiation, or radiant energy. Nuclear radiation, or radioactivity, comes from various materials that are naturally radioactive and is also emitted during some nuclear reactions. *See also* RADIOACTIVITY.

RADIOACTIVITY. A process by which atoms of certain elements decay by emitting invisible radiation and particles from their nuclei. In the process the atoms change, and the substance becomes a different element. Radium and uranium are two well-known radioactive elements.

Radioactivity was discovered around 1896 by A. H. Becquerel, a French physicist. The term itself was coined by Marie Curie in 1898.

Exposure to radioactivity can be harmful to living beings, depending on the particular radioactive substance, the amount absorbed, and the length of exposure. The possible accidental release of radioactivity into the environment is one problem with nuclear power plants and the storage of wastes from these plants. *See also* BECQUEREL, ANTOINE HENRI; CURIE, MARIE; NUCLEAR FISSION; and URANIUM.

RADIO WAVES. A form of radiant energy, somewhat similar to light. Radio waves can travel through empty space at a speed of about 186,000 miles (300,000 km) per second.

RADWASTE. *See* NUCLEAR WASTE.

RECLAMATION. The process of returning to use or to good condition. The word is used mostly to describe the method used to restore land damaged by the strip mining of coal. The reclamation process includes smoothing and grading the land, covering it with topsoil, and planting it with crops or trees. *See also* STRIP MINING.

RECYCLING. Using a material, saving it, reprocessing it, and then using it again for the same or a similar purpose. Among the most important products for recycling are metal, glass, and paper.

It requires much less energy to process and reuse waste products than to manufacture the products anew. For example, it takes 20 percent less energy to collect a used aluminum can and make it into a new one than to manufacture a totally new can.

Recycling of aluminum is important for energy conservation.

This seemingly endless maze of pipes is typical of a modern petroleum refinery.

REFINERY. An industrial plant that purifies and separates crude oil into its chemical components. The process is called cracking. The crude oil is heated, changing the chemical compounds it contains into gases. By cooling these gases and treating them in various ways, different types of gasolines and fuels are produced. Lubricants, paraffin, kerosene, asphalt, and tar are also made in the refinery.

RELATIVITY. A theory published by Albert Einstein in 1905 showing that energy and matter are related. The theory is expressed in the form of the most famous equation of science, $E = MC^2$. In words, the equation means that energy is equal to mass times the speed of light squared. Nuclear energy is an example of a reaction in which there is a loss of mass and the consequent release of energy. *See also* EINSTEIN, ALBERT; and NUCLEAR FISSION.

RENEWABLE ENERGY SOURCES. Sources of energy that are constantly being created or renewed in a relatively short period of time. Solar, wind, and water energy and energy from plant material are examples of renewable energy sources. The fossil fuels, on the other hand, are energy sources that are not renewable.

RUTHERFORD, ERNEST (1871–1937). Born in New Zealand, Rutherford worked mostly in England, where he made many important contributions to early nuclear science. He determined the structure of the atom, discovered protons and alpha and beta particles, and offered the first explanation of radioactivity. Rutherford was awarded the 1908 Nobel prize in chemistry.

**Ernest Rutherford,
1871–1937**

S

SCRUBBER. A device in the smokestack over a coal fire that removes sulfur from the smoke. It helps to cut the air pollution caused by burning coal.

SEMICONDUCTOR. A material that conducts electricity better than an insulator, but not as well as an electric wire. Solar cells are made from semiconductor materials. *See also* SOLAR CELL.

SHALE OIL. *See* OIL SHALE.

SILICON SOLAR CELL. A cell made of silicon that changes sunlight directly into electricity. Also called photovoltaic cell. *See also* SOLAR CELL.

SOLAR CELL. A device that changes sunlight directly into electricity.

A solar cell is usually made of two thin layers of silicon to which tiny amounts of other elements have been added. When the sunlight strikes the cell, it causes electricity to flow between the two layers.

Each solar cell produces only a tiny amount of electricity. Therefore, many cells are usually linked together to create a useful amount. One panel or several panels of connected solar cells is called an array.

Here, banks of solar cells are being used to power an experimental irrigation project in Nebraska.

Solar cell arrays are already in use. They were developed for spacecraft to provide electrical power, and this remains one of their major uses. They also furnish remote areas—lighthouses, isolated cabins, etc.—with electricity, power lights, and road signs.

Solar cells have no moving parts and thus don't often break down. They can also last a long time. There are several problems, however. At best, they are only about 12 to 14 percent efficient in converting the energy of sunlight into electric power. They are also expensive to produce and have limited use in areas where there may not be enough daily sunlight to guarantee a constant electrical supply. It is hoped that additional research will bring down costs and make solar-cell use more practical in the future.

Scientists are considering placing giant solar power satellites in space. These satellites, covered with solar cells and orbiting at a height of about 21,750 miles (35,000 km), could get light from the sun twenty-four hours a day. This would provide electricity even when it is cloudy on earth. A microwave transmitter linked to the satellite would beam the electricity in the form of microwaves to a control station on earth. Here the microwaves would be changed back to electrical energy and used in the same way as electricity from an ordinary power plant.

SOLAR COLLECTOR. The part of a solar energy system that collects the sun's rays, or radiant energy, and changes this energy into heat.

The most common solar collector is the greenhouse. The sun shines through the glass or plastic cover and heats the air, plants, and ground. This heat is trapped inside the greenhouse. All solar collectors work on this same basic principle.

A simple solar collector that is widely used for heating buildings and water is the flat-plate collector, which consists of a rectangular-shaped, shallow box covered by a transparent material such as clear plastic. The bottom of the box is usually a metal plate painted black to absorb the sun's energy and change it to heat. It is also insulated to help keep the heat from escaping. This solar heat can also be used for cooling by means of a special type of air conditioner.

A different type of solar collector is known as a concentrating collector. This type uses mirrors or lenses to reflect or focus the sun's rays on a dark surface, or absorber. This collector produces higher temperatures than the flat-plate collector and can be used in solar power plants to produce electricity or for industrial applications requiring hot water or steam.

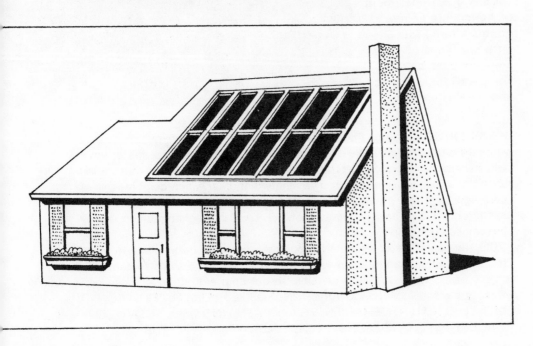

On this U.S. Department of Agriculture animal genetics farm, four different types of solar collectors are being compared for efficiency and durability.

SOLAR ENERGY. Energy that comes from the sun. Solar energy takes many different forms. The sun's heat is used to heat buildings. By means of solar cells, its light can be used to produce electricity. The light and heat from the sun are also vital to plant growth. The plants that grew hundreds of millions of years ago are today's fossil fuels, such as coal, oil, and natural gas. These fuels are burned for energy. Plants growing now can be changed into energy by biomass conversion.

The sun heats the air differently around the world, causing winds to blow. This air movement can be used as an energy source. The sun also heats the world's water, which makes it possible to get energy from water in several ways. *See also* BIOMASS CONVERSION; FOSSIL FUELS; HYDROELECTRIC ENERGY; OCEAN THERMAL ENERGY; PHOTOSYNTHESIS; SOLAR CELL; TIDAL ENERGY; WAVE ENERGY; WIND ENERGY; and WIND TURBINE.

SOLAR ENERGY SYSTEM. A system for collecting, storing, and using solar energy for space heating, cooling, or water heating. There are two basic types of solar energy systems: active systems, in which an additional source of energy is needed to distribute the solar energy; and passive systems, in which no additional pumping or transfer agent is needed. *See also* ACTIVE SOLAR ENERGY SYSTEM and PASSIVE SOLAR ENERGY SYSTEM.

SOLAR FURNACE. A device that produces very high temperatures by using a number of large mirrors to focus the sun's radiation on a single point. Often the mirrors are heliostats, built to turn and follow the sun. A solar furnace in Odeillo, France, creates enough heat to melt steel.

SOLAR HOUSE. A house built to use solar energy. The energy is used in various ways, such as heating, cooling, and producing hot water. The heat produced from solar energy is sometimes stored in large tanks of water or in

This house in Maryland uses passive solar energy concepts to provide indoor heating and cooling. Windows on the south-facing wall let winter sunlight warm the stone floor of the main living area, which is below the ground. In summer, the windows are opened to let the air in. This air rises and exits through the cathedral ceiling, creating a natural ventilation pattern.

an area filled with loose rocks. Then, when the heat is needed, it is drawn from the water or the rocks. Solar houses are most practical in areas that have many hours of continuous sunshine every year.

SOLAR POWER SATELLITE. A satellite placed in orbit around the earth that uses solar cells to change solar energy into electrical energy, then beams the electrical energy in the form of microwaves to earth. *See also* SOLAR CELL.

SOUND ENERGY. The energy produced by the rapid shaking back and forth, or vibrating, of some material. These vibrations cause waves to form in the air, which are received by the ears as sound.

STEAM. Water that has been changed from a liquid state into a gas. Steam is invisible. So-called clouds of steam are usually tiny particles of liquid water that come from steam that has been cooled.

Steam fills more space than the water from which it is made. That is why it builds up strong pressure when it is confined to a limited space. That pressure is great enough to turn the blades of a turbine in an electric power plant.

STORAGE BATTERY. *See* BATTERY.

STRIP MINING. A method of mining that is used to remove coal located near the surface. The earth and rock above the coal are stripped away, exposing the coal seam. After the coal is taken out of the ground, the material that had been dug up is dumped back. This sometimes leaves ugly scars on the landscape.

SUN. The star at the center of our solar system and the most important source of the earth's energy.

Like all other stars, the sun produces energy by the nuclear fusion that is always going on in its interior. This energy radiates outward in all directions. The earth receives only a tiny fraction of the sun's so-called radiant energy, mostly in the form of heat and light. Yet this energy is estimated to equal about 4,200 trillion kilowatts every single day. *See also* NUCLEAR FUSION.

SURFACE MINING. *See* STRIP MINING.

SYNCRUDE. Another name for liquefied coal. *See also* COAL LIQUEFACTION.

SYNTHETIC FUEL. Any fuel source created by human beings rather than found in nature. Most of the synthetic fuels are either gases or liquid fuels made from coal, such as synthetic natural gas or ethanol. Synthetic natural gas and other synthetic fuels are also made from conversion of plant material or organic wastes. These are sometimes called biomass fuels. Fuels obtained from oil shale and tar sands are also occasionally classified as synthetic fuels. *See also* BIOMASS CONVERSION; COAL GASIFICATION; COAL LIQUEFACTION; OIL SHALE; and TAR SANDS.

T

TAR SANDS. Formations of sand that contain large amounts of thick, tarlike oil. Scientists are seeking a practical way to remove this source of oil from the sand.

Tar sands are very sticky and hard to handle. They gum up and destroy machinery. Also, they are usually located far beneath the surface of the earth, and thus strip mining cannot be used. The most common approach is to extract the oil underground (*in situ*) and then pump it up.

The largest tar sand field is in Alberta Province, Canada. It contains an estimated 600 billion barrels (95 billion kl) of oil.

The tar sands in the United States are mostly in and around the state of Utah. Experts estimate that 25 billion barrels (4 billion kl) of oil are located there.

TELLER, EDWARD (b. 1908). Hungarian-born American physicist whose work at the Los Alamos Laboratory in New Mexico led to the development of the first hydrogen fusion bomb in 1952.

Teller was educated in Germany and came to the United States in 1935. He contributed much to our understanding of radioactivity and other aspects of nuclear physics.

TENNESSEE VALLEY AUTHORITY (TVA). A federal corporation created by Congress in 1933 to develop the resources of the Tennessee Valley, which covers an area of over 40,000 square miles (1 million hectares). Among the many important projects undertaken was the construction of more than forty dams on the Tennessee River and its branches. This provides hydroelectric power throughout the valley and surrounding areas, as well as controlling floods and improving navigation.

THERMONUCLEAR REACTION. *See* NUCLEAR FUSION.

THETA PINCH. A magnetic confinement device used in producing energy from nuclear fusion. *See also* MAGNETIC CONFINEMENT.

THREE MILE ISLAND. *See* NUCLEAR FISSION.

TIDAL ENERGY. Energy produced from the rise and fall of the ocean tides.

A dam is built across a bay or inlet on an ocean coast. This separates the bay or inlet from the open ocean. Set in the dam are turbines. The turbines are driven both as the tidal water flows in and as it flows out. Usually it is necessary to dig a tidal pool to hold the water at high tide and release it at low tide.

Tidal energy has two major drawbacks. One is the very high cost of building the tidal basins and dams. Also, construction of such dams may damage the environment.

The world's largest tidal power plant is located at the mouth of the River Rance in France. The river empties into the French side of the English Channel. This plant was completed in the 1960s at a cost of nearly $100 million.

The construction includes a 2,460-foot-long (750-m) dam and a tidal pool that holds 6 billion cubic feet (170 billion cubic liters) of water. It has twenty-four generators, which can produce 500,000 kilowatts of electricity. This meets the power needs of a city of 250,000 inhabitants.

When electrical demand is low, the turbines pump water into the tidal pools. This increases the amount of water that flows out as the tide is falling.

TIDES. The rise and fall of the sea. Tides are caused mostly by the gravitational pull of the moon. They rise and fall roughly twice each day. Some of the highest tides on earth are found in the Bay of Fundy on Canada's Atlantic coast. The difference between high and low tide can be as much as 50 feet (15 m). *See also* TIDAL ENERGY.

TOKAMAK. A nuclear fusion confinement system. In the Tokamak the plasma is contained in a large doughnut shape by magnetic fields. The word comes from the Russian name for the device. *See also* MAGNETIC CONFINEMENT and NUCLEAR FUSION.

TOTAL ENERGY HOUSE. A house built to conserve energy. Such a house will incorporate both active and passive solar energy systems in its construction. It will be built to take advantage of alternate energy sources, including solar cells and a windmill to provide electricity. Some total energy houses are built partly underground to use the soil to prevent wide variations in temperature. *See also* ACTIVE SOLAR ENERGY SYSTEM; ALTERNATE ENERGY SOURCES; PASSIVE SOLAR ENERGY SYSTEM; SOLAR CELL; SOLAR ENERGY SYSTEM; and WINDMILL.

TRITIUM. A type of hydrogen atom that contains one proton and two neutrons in its nucleus. Ordinary hydrogen atoms have only one proton and no neutrons in the nucleus. Deuterium, another type of hydrogen, has one proton and one neutron. The nuclei of tritium and deuterium are used as the fuel for nuclear fusion. *See also* NUCLEAR FUSION.

TURBINE. A wheel-like machine that is driven by the pressure of water, steam, or air. Windmills and waterwheels are examples of simple turbines. In most electric power plants a steam-driven turbine causes the generator to rotate, producing electricity. *See also* WIND TURBINE and WINDMILL.

TVA. *See* TENNESSEE VALLEY AUTHORITY.

URANIUM. A radioactive element that is used as a fuel in nuclear fission reactors. The isotope of uranium that is used in reactors is uranium 235, with 92 protons and 143 neutrons in its nucleus. *See also* RADIOACTIVITY.

Uranium ore, which is mined for use in nuclear power plants, is radioactive.

UTILITIES. The companies that produce and sell electricity, gas, or water. The electric utility companies build and own the power plants where the electricity is generated. They decide how to design the plant and what type of fuel to use. In making their decisions, they consider cost, availability of fuel, safety, and effect on the environment.

WATERWHEEL. An old device for changing flowing or falling water into mechanical energy. The waterwheel is basically a wheel with either paddles or cups around the rim. The water turns the wheel, and the wheel can then turn other machines.

WATT. A unit of power. *See* POWER.

WATT, JAMES (1736–1819). Scottish engineer who built the first practical steam engine, which he patented in 1769. The basic unit of electrical power, the watt, is named in his honor.

**James Watt,
1736–1819**

WAVE ENERGY. Obtaining energy from ocean waves. Wave energy is still in the early stages of development.

One promising design uses a number of hollow iron spheres built around a platform far out at sea. The upward and downward movement of the waves raises and lowers the spheres. This energy is used to lift water up to the level of the platform. Then the water is allowed to flow down, turning turbines and electric generators as it falls.

One major problem with wave energy is that of getting the electricity from platforms at sea to land, where it is needed. A solution may be to use the electricity right at the platform, perhaps for mining and refining metals from the bottom of the sea.

WIND ENERGY. Energy that comes from the movements of the air, or the blowing of the wind. Wind energy is usually produced by windmills or wind turbines.

Wind energy is a form of solar energy. The sun warms some parts of the earth more than others. Because of differences in pressure, the air from the cooler places tends to rush in to where the air is warmer. This causes a wind. The wind turns the blades or sails of any windmill in its path. The spinning of the windmill can then be used to produce electricity or do other kinds of work.

Wind energy is still not a completely practical source of energy. The wind does not always blow when and where the energy is needed. Also, a single windmill produces only a small amount of electricity. *See also* WIND TURBINE and WINDMILL.

WIND TURBINE. A machine that uses moving air to produce energy or do work.

Windmills are a very old type of wind turbine. Wind turbines today come in many different shapes and sizes. Some have long blades that look like airplane propellers set atop tall towers. Others have many narrow metal strips and look like big bicycle wheels.

The vertical axis wind turbine is a windmill that is shaped like an eggbeater. The advantage of this shape over the propeller shape is that it can capture wind from any direction. The device is inexpensive, lightweight, and high in energy output. It is being tested as one of the most promising types of wind turbines. One popular kind is named after its inventor, G. J. M. Darrieus of France, who built the first ones in the 1920s.

The basic principle of all wind turbines is the same. The blowing wind turns the blades. The energy is then used to generate electricity or do other work, such as grinding grain, pumping water, or running factory machines.

The world's largest wind turbine was built in Vermont in 1941. It was a propeller-type machine, with a 175-foot (53-m) blade that produced 1,250 kilowatts. It was used for over three years before the blade broke. *See also* WIND ENERGY.

Windmills

Traditional   *Modern*

WINDMILL. An older name for wind turbine. Windmills are machines with blades or sails that are turned by the wind. The energy of the spinning blades can be used to do work. The first windmills were built in the seventh century. They were used to mill grains and pump water.

WORK. The product of a force times the distance over which the force acts. Work is measured in foot-pounds (1 pound of force over a distance of 1 foot) or in joules (1 newton of force over a distance of 1 meter).